Sally Albiso Award Judge's Comments

Written with the discernment of koans, *Tender Currencies*—a narrative of climate, location, and geologic and human transformations—struck me with its lush language, steady rhythms, and exquisite descriptions. Here is a work of close observations of species, land formations, and internal reflections that honor healing and reconciliation, while also seamlessly incorporating the personal: family history and a dazzling finale of love poems.

—Risa Denenberg, author of
slight faith and *Rain/Dweller* and
Sally Albiso Award Judge

Tender Currencies

Tender Currencies

Scot Siegel

MoonPath Press
Sally Albiso Award Series

Copyright © 2025 Scot Siegel
All rights reserved.

No part of this publication may be reproduced, distributed, or transmitted in any form or by any means whatsoever without written permission from the publisher, except in the case of brief excerpts for critical reviews and articles. All inquiries should be addressed to MoonPath Press.

Poetry
ISBN 979-8-9899487-7-2
Revised Edition

Cover art: *Swimming Chewaucan (extinct) & Michigan*
by Scot Siegel

Author photo: Scot Siegel

Book design by Tonya Namura,
using Hypatia Sans Pro (display)
and Gentium Book Basic (text)

MoonPath Press, an imprint of Concrete Wolf Poetry Series, is dedicated to publishing the finest poets living in the U.S. Pacific Northwest.

MoonPath Press
c/o Concrete Wolf
PO Box 2220
Newport, OR 97365-0163

MoonPathPress@gmail.com

http://MoonPathPress.com

*For my sister, Stacey,
daughters, Caroline and Lianne,
and my love, Kristin.*

Your job is to find what the world is trying to be.

—William Stafford

Table of Contents

Prologue
Vista	5

High Country
High Country	9
A Paved Path	10
Transpiration	12
Climate Song	13
Coronis Fritillary	14
Great Basin	15
Out Here	16
Home Ground	17
Confluence	19
Pair of Greens	21
Snow	22
Ramona Falls	23
We Fill Our Pockets	24
Earthshine	25
Battery Low, Getting Dark	26
The Blue Whale and Her Diamonds	27

Closing Doors Softly
Enough Is Enough	31
Grandpa's Gun	32
The Day Father's Shop Burned to the Ground	33
Library	37
Blue Water	38
Without Supervision	40
While Waiting for Vaccines	41
Succulent Ornamentation	42
The Golden Mean	43
Four Tenses	44
History, the Homemaker	45
Lifting Lockdown	47

Time, the Hitchhiker	48
Teamwork	49
Closing Doors Softly	50

Bringing You Home

The Amulet	53
Bringing You Home	54
Lake Effect	55
Patient and Helper	56
Parhelion (Sundog)	58
Driving Home from Work	59
Roadside Memo, Jasmine	60
After a Light Summer Rain	62
Stowaway	63
Fender's Blues	64
Samsara	65
Our Own Private Alaska	67
Terroir of Sorrel	68
Tender Currencies	69
The Rest of Our Lives	71
Roadside Stew	72
For a Moment	74

Epilogue

Coda (Anthem)	79
Acknowledgements	81
Gratitude	83
About the Author	85

Tender Currencies

Prologue

Vista

You have travelled long enough,
loved and failed, come home
and left for other states.
You must be tired, friend.
No one else on the highway.
Lift your foot from the gas
and roll onto the shoulder.
Turn off the engine, and step
outside. This is your homecoming
and disappearing act. Turn
your back to the mountains
and look out: solace and desolation
tango on a desert playa.
This could be a new way to see
yourself in the world. Now,
give yourself permission.

High Country

High Country

I need to find a different line of work,
one that measures progress in footfall,

elevation gain and descent, through transects
of biome and microclimate; hurried season of bees

and hummingbirds holding summer's frame still
at eye level; wildflower sex at the speed of glacial till

and glaciers clinging still to the craggy roof of the world—
I could make a career of camp setup and takedown,

scouting food cache and unmapped spring,
tracking huckleberries and morels; wading cool currents

gathered in a loose shirt; casting with Aengus's brown
topless girl who divines bull trout

from an emerald pool with a cane pole and red berry—
I must begin and end each day like this

beside a ring of river stone, feasting on a small
steely fire of my own making.

A Paved Path

> *If I speak for the earth I must sing.*
> —Eva Saulitis

This nature park, nearly as large
as the hole in the heart of the forest

that was originally here, holds black-
tailed deer, coyotes, and maybe a cougar.

Twisted mole-bone-and-fur scat
litter the verge, and splotches of

hawthorn berries mark my walk.
Lazuli buntings flounce upon the willows

and graze on cinnabar caterpillars
ravaging the tansy ragwort.

Blue-faced, copper-chested, weighing
less than this pencil, buntings sing

a sweet-swishing-melodic-squeegee song
pine top to pine top. They know more about

fickle jet streams and ocean warming than
hundreds of weather apps.

In the afterwork-human-crush-for-
fresh-air, I must get my steps in

and take good care of this heart
that limps along like an old black lab.

Not complaining; I live in this world,
and therefore have a high pain threshold.

There is too much at stake; we think we are
not always free to love, yet buntings await.

At this moment, some blaze through the oaks
unbeknownst to those on electric bicycles.

I do my part, keep my head on a swivel,
and try not to look down at my phone so much.

Transpiration

—Graham Oaks Nature Park, Wilsonville, Oregon

Even on a fierce day like this,
hottest year on record, the preserve

a parched clattering of stunted oaks,
brittle fescue, and burnt Junegrass,

a breeze foretells Earth's tilt, delighting
the cabbage white butterfly, an invasive

whose rice-paper wings arch inside
an umbel of Queen Anne's lace, also invasive—

Now a loose strand of wind teases thousands
of tiny florets that shiver like stars or snow,

and the sentinel oaks know,
there are no happy or sad endings

to this story that moves water
from one delicate body to another.

Climate Song

She keeps daffodil bulbs in the freezer
and never plants them.

Spring knocks earlier each year
but withers into summer before it can begin.

Wildfire ash accumulates like snow
until November rains wash it away.

Winter comes in episodic tantrums,
with hail verging on snow before

railing back to rain; a year's worth
of rain in ten days.

She resists, an essential little act:
scions of forsythia and quince

bloom from a crystal vase
placed in the shop-front window.

Coronis Fritillary

—for the Cowiche Canyon Conservancy

Why is gravity stronger on a
railroad trestle?

Is it due to the airy space
or the molecular weight of creosote?

Does vertigo know the long wait
for trains that no longer pass

through an andesite canyon
or the patchwork of easements

and fee-simple deeds the Cowiche
Conservancy manages now?

How much weight in the spotted
butterfly's careening dive

for yellow blossoms of rabbitbrush
blooming through the ballast?

Great Basin

Here, ribs protrude soft belly
between basin and range.

It's nip-and-tuck beneath
shifting bolts of corduroy.

Is lightning a rhetorical argument
between flowers and wind?

I held a vision: a snowline inverted,
the sky smirched crimson and gray…

When the vision faded
my palms ached,

my feet burned blue.
If this country has no army

why does rabbitbrush
make my nose twitch?

Out Here

—after Ursula Le Guin

Coyote froze in perpetual leap-the-
razor-wire pose.

You cannot own a desert, but hard water
will lease to you.

You fishtail off-road, the sky snares you
with its laugh.

You conjure antelope hoofs strike alkali flats
like matchsticks

they kick up the brine shrimp and you
lick the bitter crust.

You heard there is a diner, but the herd
has wandered.

Steens means laughter while longing for
a steak.

When a fake creek swells you
overcorrect.

Three crows make a raven repairing the road;
nine ripen a heron loose from the reeds;

                                but a heron here
is a tame pterodactyl, a living fossil—

the desert is not an island
but an inland sea.

Home Ground

—*after Lake Tahoe*

July 4

Here we dive from a granite boulder
into the frigid womb, then rise like krill

to the surface. We cannot help but kick
harder than necessary in 40°F water.

Sixteen hundred feet below our pale toes,
something lurking, our hearts thumping

like the rusted gears of the Earth's cartilage,
or the memory of what created us.

Labor Day

Pines know the smell of their own kind
burning.

Under the trestles of windy ridges,
like anemones,

they feel blindly, smoke writhing;
they read it like Braille.

Thanksgiving

After years of drought, record snowfall
defies the almanac.

The body of the lake feels nostalgic;
kisses touching down, and the storm

singing through the night,
like the spaces between songs

on dusty vinyl records. You keep
lifting the needle, replaying my favorites.

Passover

I linger below grade, listening for fissures
in the cool cellar

that is my sickness.

Through a portal called spring
snowmelt torques the birches, a wet ratchet.

When winter blanket melts, the basement oozes
a wet wool smell, a girlish tincture—

then mountains rise, pulling apart roads,
cables, gas lines...

High in the aspen chorus of my childhood,
power poles lean and sing.

Confluence

—for the McKenzie River Trust

I was prepared for the bitterness of creosote
when I plucked the one with mustard wings,

black rings, and red spots around the eye.
When I smudged it

and rubbed the sticky residue over my thumb
I felt the warmth and weight of a century

between the Kalapuya roasting tarweed seed
on a gravel bed, salmon pushing upriver,

and the abandoned quarry-turned-muddy-
conservancy-land-transfer.

Tarweed grows wildly, if sparingly,
on the toe-slope of white oak savannah.

I am snapping pictures of flowers
when Holly points at the gate, and says,

*We could use more eyes on the site.
The climate is changing, migrating north,*

and her gaze at the land is deeper than time,
when she says, *Black might be better*

than white oak for the future ecological plan;
better adapted to shifting latitudes.

I am searching for an eddy now, a quiet spot
where I might glimpse a great blue heron

or the brown blur of an otter in the glimmer
of midday sun. But the river is a straight shot;

the BPA easement bisects riparian swath
under the hum of power transmission lines.

Public access is prohibited, but the Trust is
working on that; they have a vision:

Educational programming, sitting-in-nature
while being Black, Brown, or Indigenous;

stewardship as inclusive access, experiential
learning.

Here, where the Middle and Coast Forks meet,
is the confluence of trust and reconciliation,

reconnecting to natural systems, repair
and adaptation. This is where the healing begins—

Trust in the un-straightening of rivers
Trust in the sweet labor of volunteers

Trust when they breach the dike for
beavers, nature's master engineers

Trust in the river's muscle, heart, and lungs—
I should not have been surprised

by the diligence and patience of the Trust,
or the gentle citrus scent of tarweed.

Pair of Greens

Vampirish in dark capes, they stalk
damselflies at wetland's edge

and hunt from clumps of sedge
or stumps for higher ground

on account of their stout build
and hunched posture on twig legs.

Not egrets or bitterns, more sarcastic.
Not regal like their blue cousins

though juveniles don a splash of sun,
splotches on subdued plumage.

Better light reveals rainforest-
green backs, chanterelle-brown necks

and breasts, and slate-gray wings,
which on takeoff unfold akimbo.

Midflight, their necks might appear
unwieldy, though on the ground

green herons stalk smooth as a pop
star's moonwalk.

We approach, and they let us get close
staying focused on the next meal.

On each side of a clawlike beak,
a little sunstone eye—

in that fierce glare at the dragonfly,
you might recognize a hint of pterodactyl.

Snow

The Inuit have many
names for you, most I cannot
pronounce. So let's keep it
simple and call you Snow.

You always seem to know
when I am here. You do not
speak, but eavesdrop
through office windows.

When I move to the next
room, you are there.
I change floors, and
there you are again.

What are you trying to
say? Is it something
about how the world
began, or how it ends?

Snow, I place my hand
on the glass, and try
in good faith; I want
to understand,

but your language
is difficult, so many
vowels, far more than rain,
a dialect nearer to love.

Ramona Falls

I cannot look at those jade-laced
        falls in the Cascade Mountains
                without falling in love.

Here, Ramona spits
        icy sheets at our faces—
                we make a nice bed on her moss.

The froth of her breath is a long
        kiss; we cannot resist
                such pleasure!

Ridiculous, I know, personifying
        wilderness, a waterfall—

but what is love
        if not a free fall

        forestalled,

high above the rapids?

We Fill Our Pockets

—after Caroline, age 9

All things, even the rocks, make a little noise.
—William Stafford

You are in bed hiding.
A storm of your own making
builds outside the window.
Dreams, like bats, tug our tents
and browse the yard.

We are geologists.
We fill our pockets
with carnelian agates
and less beautiful
specimens: clamshells

split and riddled by
sea lice. False fossils.
Bits of iron slag
we haul in T-shirt rucksacks
from the shoreline.

We hold our currency close,
talismans to ward off
nightmares, and stranger
premonitions. We care
for stones like brittle birds

the way I care for these words—
little glass origami
I carry down the mountain
to tell you someday.

Earthshine

When Venus and Jupiter align
in the near sky

look to the right, and you might spot
a blue-gray rind

interposed between sunlit crescent
and the slightly darker sky—

Old Moon
in the New Moon's arms.

Battery Low, Getting Dark

—after Discovery (2004–2018)

Was it the dual moons,
Phobos and Deimos,
that made you sing?

Or that furtive lake
tucked like a heart
in the chest of Mars?

Discovery, you are
dead to us now.
Another rover

has taken over.
She tries reading the
mind of the Red Planet.

Have you seen *Curiosity*?
If your paths cross,
tell her Chandra's on

the chopping block,
and not to attempt
Mt. Sharp.

Tell me, have you found
a cure for dust storms
of the heart?

The Blue Whale and Her Diamonds

> *Voyager's message is carried by a phonograph record,*
> *a 12-inch gold-plated copper disk containing sounds*
> *and images selected to portray the diversity of life*
> *and culture on Earth.*
> —NASA Jet Propulsion Laboratory

Voyager reaches deep into space, the deepest ever,
the junior news anchor reports. But I think he means, *Yet*,
because isn't the universe expanding, all matter
projecting from one vertex, on a radial course
for discovery, if not destiny?

Voyager drifts deeper toward infinity, traversing
interstellar space, yet is unable to procreate.
What makes this vessel more significant than the rest?
The zebra mussel hitches a ride from Korea to Seattle
in the bilge of a ship. A real pioneer. And a corner of

the wharf a tsunami ripped loose crosses the Pacific
with an aquarium of radioactive fish in its cavity—
Space Station right here on earth. There is a strange
grace in the blinding of *Voyager*, infrared spectrometer
and radiometer shut down for now. I don't like space junk

obscuring the night sky, ghost nets strangling puffins,
or islands of plastic clogging the intestines of the largest
animals on earth. It is difficult to sort out. I'd like to believe,
stars twinkle not from a child's wish, or a mother's prayer,
or the air itself obscured by pollution,

but the unending stream of unknown particles coming
between us and them; micro-shards of galactic mass;
bits of stone, iron, and glass; and traces of oxygen
and ice. I love how they disrupt the light
and make the dark sky dance.

Closing Doors Softly

Enough Is Enough

Stop with the billionaire space probes
and turn down the ocean.

We come into this world the same
as we leave, squinting and suckling.

Don't talk to me about lunar governance
or the preponderance of evidence

that water can be extracted from asteroids
or the Moon.

If you ask where I am going, *Heaven or Hell?*
I choose Venus.

I would like to believe there is a special place
for you and me,

a warm spot on her marble lap,
to rest our heads.

Grandpa's Gun

Retrieve it from a dry, dark place.
Pull it from a sleeve, some feltlike leather
with our name inscribed on a flimsy tag.
Examine it for any trace of him.

This was a gift to my father from his true father,
the one with spaniels and a hunting lodge,
not the one we could not speak of.
I take up the heft, and get the sense

I am looking down the long barrel of
some unknown history. He'd always tell me,
Safety on, until you're absolutely ready.
Watch your stance; hold steady.

I scan the room. No window. No door.
Just the gun like an iron dove in my hand.
With love, I turn it over, brush my fingers along
the stock, find his initials in smooth silver ridges.

Turn over again, and drink from a spring called
The pooling of history, a chalice of blood, Chernihiv
forests at dusk... I have his chin, when I lift and pump
the muzzle, his shoulder when I place it in the crook,

his eyes pressing cold metal to my face.
Then his voice, when something faint
and terrible in the shape of my real name
burns through the cheekpiece.

The Day Father's Shop Burned to the Ground

—after Hiam Mosher "George" Livchitz

When I'm afraid, I don't think of something my father said.
I think of poppies, and the wild almond trees on the hill
behind our house; and in those years before I became
a Bar Mitzvah, there was a game:
Hide-and-Seek in the Dark.

Once, when it was my turn to find the others, I hid
and kept counting. For a long time, I thought
I'd never be found; it was getting dark, and I grew
hungry. With a rock I crushed the velvet husk
of an almond, only to find it shriveled and bitter inside.

Far below my hiding place, the dark bay divided
our hills from the city. In the distance, San Francisco
pulsed and bloomed through a lens of fog
and pollution; a luminescent field of poppies.

Inside that shell, the old industrial district,
a sanctuary for immigrants south of Market,
and my father's print shop on Ninth Street.
The air inside was a stew of ink,

sweat, cigarettes, and hot metal; ammonia
trays a gaunt man leaned over all day
in the darkroom, proofing negatives,
burning silver plates in solitude.

Summers, when the men were under a deadline,
I went with my father. I remember the bitter
smell, burnt coffee wafting like taxidermy
from the west end of the bridge to the sweatshop

where Irishmen, Mexicans, Chinese, Blacks
and the great-grandson of a Russian rabbi
worked side by side collating and stacking
gloss pages of high-fashion catalogues,
gluing fabric to cardstock.

Eight years old, I thought this was the whole world.
The pressmen, heroic Irishmen, bulging
in sweat-stained T-shirts. The constant hollering
over locomotive hiss-clack-suck. Heidelbergs
chewing through reams of paper.

Under aluminum lamp swing, a ballet
when they pirouetted, cigarettes dangling,
canted away from the eyes; huge sheets of
freshly inked paper hefted to the light—
then the sudden jaw-twitch release of ashes...

My salesman father, polyester sport coat, blue
striped tie, would say: *Stay away from them.
You don't want to be a pressman. Those machines,
saddle-stitchers, guillotines, will take a finger,
or an arm, in an instant.*

Though sometimes he'd soften, like after a good
pressrun, his hand steadying my shoulder, leaning over,
showing me how to feed bolts of fabric to the steaming-hot
swatch-backing machine. Pressmen looked on, smiling
through ink-stained teeth.

Then there was Mrs. Hickey. She was never happy.
Even after a good pressrun, she'd be carrying on over
something, yelling at my father about some customer,
or money. She ruled the place with a temper that rivaled
the presses; unpredictable around children, I thought
she just hated Jews.

My mother heard from a neighbor who had been watching
the evening news, the building went in less than two hours.
Oil and ink boiled, and the two-ton Heidelbergs burned
through two floors to the basement. Firemen found a pool
of molten metal on concrete slab. The *Chronicle* said,
One in a string of five arsons.

Dismal was dinner that night; mother slowly twirling
in front of the oven, wrapped in telephone cord. I knew
it was a time. Something about insurance and grandfather.
San Francisco-by-way-of-Shanghai grandfather. Son-of-a-
Russian-orthodox-rabbi grandfather. Family-fled-
Bolshevik-persecution grandfather...

Once, I asked for Grandpa's birthday:
Was he alive during the earthquake?

Maybe 1909 or '12, Mother said,
Not even he knows for sure.

Then a feeling came over me
that I had never felt before; a black cape
when she said, *Go. Just go outside and play.*

It had grown dark, and the hills made a forlorn sound.
Some bay winds turned upslope and found me—
For a long time, I shiver under the almond tree,
hunched in the dirt alone, turning over stones:

> *What are we going to do?*
> *Will my father have the answer?*
> *Will they take our home?*

Then, I felt a great surge, a heartbeat stirred
among the rocks and grasses—

    I pressed my ear to the ground
and heard the steady taproot pulse
of a great clock whirring,
and his voice:

> *With love, You sustain the living*
> *With great compassion give life to all*
> *You send help to the falling*
> *and healing to the sick*
> *You bring freedom to the captive*
> *and keep faith with those who sleep in the dust.* [1]

Then I lowered my hands,
and turned to face the world.

---

[1] From the Hebrew prayer, *T'Filah-Amida* (*G'vurot*—"Powers")

Library

At a certain age
it is strange walking
the Earth, as an adult,
among other adults
who were not here
even as babies
when you were a child.

You peer down the aisles
where you once stood,
see those you knew
replaced by children
sitting cross-legged, smiling,
not a care in the world,
immersed in books.

Blue Water

—after Ann "Fritzie" Siegel

At thirteen, I'd get up at five
and walk through the city
to the causeway above Biscayne Bay
and sight-fish for sheepshead.

I never told you, didn't want you to worry,
but I met this guy who kept all his belongings—
tangle of rods, tackle, sleeping bag, and tarp—
in a shopping cart. He'd talk to everyone

and no one, about the war, and the Sea of Cortez—
a favorite of expats and vagabond lovers, he'd say—
where you could pick up spiny lobsters in crystal clear
water, and barbecue them on the beach.

I could barely see over the rail, so he'd help
maneuver my bait through the waves toward the piling
where the biggest sheepshead fed on barnacles. Once,
I caught a neon-green parrotfish the size of a football.

He kept yelling, *Break it off, son! Break it off!*
But I froze in the tropical rain. A shadow under the bridge
grew as an eight-foot nurse shark curled into view
and took the parrotfish, snapping my line.

I remember how much you loved to swim in the ocean,
frilly blue bathing dress pulsing like a jellyfish in the surf.
Do you remember the school of bluefish, fierce
and yellow-eyed, that came in close to feed on mullet?

Thousands of finger-sized oily fish swerved around
my belly, bumping into your knees. *Safety in numbers*,
you'd say; and thick was that school, the ocean turning
smoky blue and flecked with silver in the frenzy.

Sometimes, the wind would kick up, and blobs of tar
stuck to our feet. You said they were from leaky tankers.
I did not understand. I thought oil came from dinosaurs,
or faults in the ocean floor.

The Bluebottle Jellyfish scared me more: "Man o' War"
whose sting can paralyze, you warned... The ocean
drew us in with its thorny charms: sharks and vets,
poisonous tentacles, and curious fish with beaks.

Without Supervision

After a hard city snow
a stiff east wind
shakes the house
like a sifter,
loosing powder,
scattering it everywhere.
The sky cracks open,

unfolds a hand,
hands over a yolk;
sun alights on a bridge,
city at a standstill.
The sky gloats like a child
who's baked Linzer torte
for the very first time.

While Waiting for Vaccines

Babies survived at a higher rate
became a year older
some not yet kissed
by a grandparent.

They waited, unvaccinated,
and not knowing
what they were missing,
giggling with puzzled eyes.

Some smiled less
than their older siblings
whose parents felt the absence
the powerlessness

the finiteness of hours,
waiting to hug *their* parents,
some of whom died alone,
memorialized in virtual services.

The days stretched
and contracted. Deer
and coyotes sauntered
down empty streets...

Who would survive?
Who would get hugged first?
Long-distance lovers too had to wait;
the virus did not discriminate.

Succulent Ornamentation

—One year into the pandemic

When the virus finally mutates
into a rain-soluble sugar,
shrivels into non-matter, and lifts off,
returning to the fourteenth century,
let's socially isolate for one more day.

First, we'll fast and be gracious
for the stars that once saved us
on the high seas and desert;
and the Moon, for its amorous pull
and nourishing tug; and the Sun too

because where would we be
without its stubborn light,
which is not preserved for us,
but for the Earth itself,
such resplendence!—

of which we are an afterthought
in a garden, some succulent
ornamentation, an aberration,
mutation, a beautiful
blip in time.

The Golden Mean

There is an alcove on the north side of the street
where no one smokes and the stucco sheds
enough heat to keep the stoops clear of ice.

On the south side, the plow leaves mounds of
frozen grit on the walk, and the wind tosses
cigarette butts against the town hall.

Inside, the three self-described *Angry Grannies*
testify against the latest development,
citing too many newcomers and downed trees.

The developer's lawyer and engineer do their best
to evade the town council's questions; their loose ties
and tight smiles hurt our teeth.

When the mayor slams the gavel at 11 p.m., the meeting's
adjourned and the Grannies file out, nudged by
the custodian's vacuum and an overstretched cord.

There will be another meeting with more discord
in two weeks, where the same folks will speak
on the same but different topics,

raising new but old questions about the town's fate;
and again the council will vote
for one side or the other.

Four Tenses

There is no present like the Present.
It is the gift that keeps on giving.

The Future offers everything, promises
nothing, and delivers something else.

The Past cannot remember what the Future
tried explaining to the Present.

Truth sometimes occurs when Past,
Present, and Future all sing in the same key.

History, the Homemaker

History is independently wealthy.
She has so many rooms, she's lost track.
History is hoarse from having to repeat herself.
She is losing her mind yet has all the time in the world.
History knows how worlds come to an end.
She lived in a convent once, but was caught revising
the scripture.
History is a math wizard and believes in home remedies.
History is not the Virgin Mary; she kicks the baby out with
the father.
History craves something savory for a late-night snack.
She hates the History Channel more than Science Fiction.
History critiques *The Great British Baking Show*,
reclining in a bath.
She barters the family jewels for bourbon and hawks the
silver for food.
History prefers cardamom to cinnamon.
When she cooks her moods swing with Jupiter's moons.
History has a habit of leaving the oven on.
She's burned the house down so many times you'd think
she does it for the rush.
When time cannot save her, she rebuilds the house
with iron and cedar and treats the linens with camphor.
History was arrested once for shooting up Fiction.
Drunk, she revises her autobiography to cheer herself up.
History knows all your secrets; she is the headmistress
at the School of Hard Knocks.
She does not wear pumps or grow her hair out for you.
History loves Allegory, and wears Paradox to the ball.
She leaves early, something boiling at home.
History cooks for armies—
She fills your plate with more than you can eat.
History knows the homeless are royalty.
She keeps the leftovers warm for centuries.

History is never alone.
Her secret lover wears the old cologne.
History leaves the door open.

Lifting Lockdown

The first day back was like
the first day of first grade

when we sat apart for the first time
and glanced at each other longer than was safe.

In that room the teacher policed
with stares not entirely her own,

we were closer to wolves
than boys and girls, which either meant

everyone was a threat, or anyone
could be your friend, depending—

and you wouldn't know
until you tried.

Time, the Hitchhiker

Time wears a red bandana and yellow flip-flops in the rain.
He likes chasing pickups and whistling at the ladies.
Time does not listen to his parents, Gravity and Inertia.
He stays out all night, and chucks the hourglass into the river.
Time is always in a hurry when you are running late.
He is the backseat driver who won't show you the map.
Time loves fast food but shuns the drive-through.
He makes you pull off at every rest stop but refuses to pee.
Time smokes while you pump the gas.
He won't offer to pay, but runs up the tab.
Grow impatient, and Time takes his sweet time.
He tags along whether you like it or not.
Time scoffs at time zones and speed limits.
He does not believe in curfews or deadlines.
Time is a stowaway on a runaway train named Time.
He flies first class, hoards the overhead storage,
and steals your snack.
Time will set you up, then send you down the river.
He loves swing dancing and erratic weather.
Time conjures picnic lightning, downpours on clotheslines.
He claims diplomatic immunity during natural disasters,
and takes the Fifth on a full solar eclipse.
Time is the vampire who sucks your time dry.
Time is a one-night stand who dines and ditches.
Whatever you do, don't feed Time or his bitches.

Teamwork

Here, Past, Present, and Future on a life raft with no paddle. Past says, *Last time, only one survivor.* But that was long ago, and no one else remembers. Future insists, *This is no joke.* The wind is picking up. Present, using his hands, paddles harder. The others have no hands. The raft spins in circles. Future says, *This could be a dark parable,* which gives Present pause. But Past has seen far worse. Beyond the horizon, Fate and Luck fight over the helm of a freighter. Truth is in the engine room, trying to figure it out, but the blueprints have faded, and the specs are written in a language similar to but different than the six spoken on this ocean.

foghorn
a woman's form
in the rain

Closing Doors Softly

I am searching for scissors in the junk drawer
when I find a note from an old friend who has passed
that says: *Had we never met, I would miss you more—*
and it jogs a memory, unlocking a door to something else
I once read: *In addition to extinct stars, whose wobbly light
continues, there are others, much nearer, but so new,
we do not see them...* On the next clear moonless night,
let's set up the beach chairs in the yard, and stare
at a swatch of sky until our eyes glass over.
I want to catch a star winking anew with you.
Some friends we'll never see again.
So many more though we have yet to meet.

in springtime
everyone secretly
loves you

Bringing You Home

The Amulet

The man falls asleep with a book on his chest.
She watches him breathe while pretending to read.
The dog on the floor twitches in its sleep.
The moon is not a moon tonight.
The man not a bachelor or widower.
The woman is not happily or unhappily married.
The dog is not a dog but nearly a wolf—
The woodstove never needs refueling.

Bringing You Home

*I've decided that when I die I get to see all my beloved
dead people and also my bird dogs that died,
if I don't fuck up.*
—Jim Harrison (1937–2016)

When I die I am going straight to Michigan to see my dad's
hunting dogs. His father's too. Maybe we'll all hunt
together, 12-gauges slung over our similarly cockeyed
shoulders, as Grandpa beats a path through ash and sumac
beside the Au Sable's black-green glare.

Maybe in that burnt-tire of a backcountry where our
parents still know each other, and some have reconciled,
dogs run from house to house lapping up food scraps and
licking our faces. Maybe they know how it is with us,
that we had to hide our love for seven lifetimes; and now
we can't help but make the furniture creak when we sleep,
and they grin when we rise from the breakfast table

satiated and still starry from the night, then glint and scurry
with mugs of coffee sloshing out to the back forty thousand
acres of state lands, where the dim and declawed revenant
moon skips over the tips of jack pines, trying to keep up
with the long train of pointers and retrievers in our wake.

Lake Effect

The night wind unwinds
rousing our neighbors' voices
The heatwave breaking

Remember the lake?
Stars swarming like caddisflies
kissing the surface?

The wind did not sleep
moving endlessly between
overheated rooms

of aspen and pine
seeking schist or granite slab
a place to lie down

Let's find some relief
slip into bathymetric daze
let the breeze barter

uncharted stars for
night swimmers far from the dock—
let minnows caress our toes

Patient and Helper

—Lianne, age 13, at Forward Stride

Thirteen, first day on
the job, with a boy
we do not know,
you stand ready,
listening:

*Use the red clicker
for catching Dancer.
If you don't know how,
ask a helper. Don't use it
on any other horse.*

*Ladybug's easy. Keep an eye
on Ruby, and don't leave
Tucker's hay soaking
anywhere near Blesi's stall.
If windy, keep Ed inside...*

A fluorescent light crackles
some crucial memorial
for late-summer insects,
as the boy who possesses
part or all of an extra

twenty-first chromosome
steps toward the unnamed
mare who shuffles and clops
in the dark rear stall.
Down syndrome children

have impaired cognitive
and physical growth
and facial characteristics
identifiable at pregnancy or birth.
Though some features appear in

persons lacking the extra chromosome:
shorter limbs, poor muscle tone,
simian crease in the palms
and that almond shape to the eyes
that can leave you guessing

about the larger-than-
normal spaces between
big and second toes;
and those extra-
wide smiles.

In the faint barn light,
you move like an angel.
Crisscrossing the aisle,
you're a hummingbird,
quick, then still,

your hand guiding
the boy's hand;
you brush Blesi down
and begin with
the hoof pick.

Quiet down there,
impossible now
to tell the differences
between patient
and helper.

Parhelion (Sundog)

—for Lianne, after winter break

At twenty-one, you climb the Santiam sled hill
as you've done so many times before,
at least in my memory, which experiences
everything you do as an endless echo.

The same gait at five, or how I remember five:
Determined, yet playful, each stride intentional.
Swing dancer, you look back every ten steps
admiring your own footwork—amplitude,

altitude—each step a bit faster. I wave, but
you do not look up. I wave again, and point,
but you do not see what I am saying. Behind you,
a sundog, an ice rainbow, skitters across

the bluest sky ever.
I meant to tell you, it was a perfect day.

Driving Home from Work

If we are the culmination of mistakes
that led us here,

in my estimation, Earth's rotation is slowing,
and that partially explains my success.

At sixteen, I'd shrug without thinking,
and like a cat squinting, exclaim, *Whatever!*

But now it feels weightier, like some kind of
doom, the wheel of time, or a grinding stone.

I try forming a smile with no teeth, saying it
under my breath, *Whatever*—and this helps.

Mistakes accumulate like microplastics;
reason becomes flightier,

unstable as a murmuration of swifts
lost in a storm, searching for a dry chimney.

Roadside Memo, Jasmine

> *The sulfur in the morning glory's juice served to vulcanize the rubber; a process antedating Charles Goodyear's discovery by at least 3,000 years.*
> —Wikipedia, "Morning glory"

I walk to work now. Gas prices
and middle age urge me onward.

Nature is aloof in lavish gardens;
Himalayan blackberry, Scotch

broom, and English ivy,
invade the last of Portland's woodlands.

Morning glories have no mercy;
they'll pull down a house, board by board,

and drag it into the river.
Though one tiny flower overtakes

the smell of truck brakes burning;
jasmine sloughs on a cedar fence

and says, *Stay for a while. Linger on my
musky breath; lick my balmy dusk.*

I plant myself on a mossy boulder,
cars whizzing by, tailpipes spewing sulfur—

mothers with strollers, landscapers,
teenagers with freshly minted licenses—

all disappear on the blind curve
ahead...

A dark wind floods the roadside gully
and what was empty quickly fills

tinctured with a Siren's scent.
She drifts over in a cobweb teddy,

fingering my hair, cupping my eyes;
she whispers through my veins like silver.

After a Light Summer Rain

Wild mint resinous in the ditch weeds
where the rubber boa, three feet long,

maybe thirty years old, plays dead
beside the trail, digesting

two moles or mice at once. Harmless,
the Fish & Wildlife app says.

Boas use their blunt tail as a decoy;
no venom, but a hit of heavy musk

when the snake suffocates its prey
before engulfing it with a wide rubber mouth.

I think I see something writhe
under the dull brown skin with tiny scales

that curl asynchronously, slowly
contracting like an outgoing tide.

Stowaway

Every night we give ourselves over
to the rudderless deep
—KB

Once, a word in a dream changed me.
Less a word than a scent or touch
it came and went with a fierce kiss.

On waking, I could not remember.
Minnows swarmed and stripped the hook;
that kiss slipped from consciousness.

Tonight, stars run deep. I settle in,
my bed a sloop, and trim the mainsheet;
let memory drift degrees downwind...

then winch it in, and beat a course
for a new continent with soft sand
and fragrant heath

where wild words still walk the land
and kiss you in your sleep.

Fender's Blues

—Marys Peak Watershed, Oregon Coast Range

At the edge of the cold firepit
where they made love the night before

two Fender's blue butterflies flit
and dive, the way some people talk,

deflecting taxonomy, not pausing long enough
to pledge allegiance to the color blue.

Barefoot with wet hair from the shower
tied back loosely in a knot, she steps through

damp larkspur to sit beside him. But the clattering
jays and crows overtake the din of creek chortle—

there is no ensemble, no serenade—
only two blue butterflies drying their wings

at the edge of the moon's thumbprint,
sipping from a bowl of ashes.

Samsara

We are on a train between Portland
and the promise of an aurora borealis

when the possibility of skating on a lake
in Michigan with you becomes real.

Yellow alder leaves gloss the mouth
of the tunnel that frames my trance

when the man assigned to sit next to me
offers to yield his seat to you.

*

Because we are new to one another, and share
the same dream of migratory cranes, few rules govern;

one is no pretense, which begets no history
no trajectory...

How you come to sit next to me is beyond me
but within reach, so I hold your hand.

A hand is a strange thing the way it thinks—
it seems to know what to do.

*

When you ask me to watch your bag, it strikes me,
I would trust you with the rest of my life.

No crush prepares us for the next, even as each
leaves an electrical charge that tastes like the past.

Some trains pull away and return empty-handed.
In a lifetime, many things do not come to pass.

Every three seconds, a plane lifts off, and the heart
drops in the moment death decides what to do.

*

That was the most loved I had ever felt, nearly
make-believe; the clouds lifting, and the pines,

weighted down with sugar snow, began to sway—
the lake exhaled through fissures in its heart

and cleared its throat. Because we are human,
we make eye contact only one soul at a time.

At night, when I close my eyes, you are skating
figure eights, waving back to me, in the lemony light.

Our Own Private Alaska

So, this is how it's done—
camp smoke and a hard nap.

We could stay here, suckle on latitude
sickness, settle into an acute

daydream: nunataks above the noon
noise, ice-clutched flags of green

auroras. How could it be so simple?
The sea stippled, though no wind,

and you and I so close, under a patch
of sky arched and aching.

Terroir of Sorrel

I follow because you know
which leaves can be eaten.

Oxalis takes on different flavors
depending on exposure and elevation.

At the intersection of oak and fir
that clover curls your lip like a poison.

But where lupine blooms under yew
a tincture of pippins tickles the tongue.

Rung by rung, the higher we climb,
the sweeter the roughage.

Tender Currencies

*What have you done on the scale
of life, and have I mattered?*

Some compose symphonies.
Others paint, or sing in the shower.

We piece together words.
You swivel your hips over a meadow

and your skirt brushes my wrist.
I write that down.

You place your hand on my chest
and press lightly; my hand

instinctually moves to your waist.
I note that too.

When our free hands meet at the curve
of your back, I drop my pen and rest there.

Sometimes, we slope into each other
like one animal dozing.

I've lost track of how many times
we've succumbed.

Now a gang of cedar waxwings
run off with my notes

and scatter my ashes over
Lake Tahoe...

If I go first, I will be sad
in a blue but content way.

If you were to love another
this strongly and gently

after I'm gone,
I would be happy for you,

but bluer than the depths
of this alpine lake.

Every day, you matter immensely;
so much so that you are

sitting across from me now
in the same room, writing this down too,

but with a slightly different lilt
in your pen, that says,

I love you in fewer words,
so deeply, this map unfolds forever.

The Rest of Our Lives

—for K

When you ask, where shall we live
and how do we afford it?

I want to say, we will be Earth-rich,
not house-poor.

We'll tend a community garden,
not a poorhouse of monthly payments.

Let us have a storehouse of wildflowers,
mountain ramblings, and seascape foraging.

Life appreciates when our dwelling moves
with the moods of weather and seasons.

I need you more than home equity.
Let's live simply, within our means,

and put the principle back in "principal."
I want to accrue it all with you.

Roadside Stew

I do not try to solve the algebraic
equation that is the red-tailed hawk

flashing across the rain-smeared
windshield, then dropping to wheel-level

and pinning its prey to the ground,
folding in on itself, growing small

and still in the rearview, like a prayer.
It is too much to bear, much less solve;

too many variables, and those large
indivisible numbers to carry—

I left my place an hour ago
and stopped for a pound of lamb.

Fifteen dollars at the bourgeois grocery
in the town where I used to live,

before the divorce, before I knew
my own worth, and the true value

of time. Time for a walk in the
woods after work with you

as Mount Talbert gives way
to the rain and dark, and we stumble

over cedars' contorted roots,
letting the stew simmer;

or weekend time in December,
nothing else to do but dip and roll

beeswax candles for the solstice,
a sabbath, or a blackout,

or for no reason at all.

For A Moment

no curve
no smoke
no drought
no death count
no invisible threat
no need for a mask
no recoil from a hand
   that only wants
your touch
your tenderness
your breaking-bread
your heaven-sent
your wishes and gifts
your latent caress
your *shhhh...*

Epilogue

Coda (Anthem)

When you are lost
let me be your island.
When thoughts go dark
I am your range of light.

When you have no words
I can be your words
like hands on sore shoulders,
cool water on a blistering day.

When you are cold, I'll be
your shawl. When overworked
I am your lunch break
or your getaway car.

When you say, *I am afraid,*
and even when you won't,
I am here for you.
If you are broke

I am a bundle of hundreds
you find on the street.
Look at me, one human
to another—

I am free for the taking
and I am taking this
moment to tell you,
I love you so.

Acknowledgements

These poems first appeared, some in earlier forms or with different titles, in the following publications:

Acorn: a Journal of Contemporary Haiku: "Foghorn"

Birdbrains: A Lyrical Guide to Washington State Birds, Raven Chronicles Press, 2025: "Pair of Greens"

The Coachella Review: "High Country"

Crab Creek Review: "History, The Homemaker"

Haibun Today: "Closing Doors Softly"

High Desert Journal: "Out Here"

Orange Linings, TriMet public art, Portland, Oregon: "In springtime"

Oregon Poetry Association Newsletter: "Lifting Lockdown," "Anthem," "Succulent Ornamentation"

Oregon Stories, Ooligan Press, Portland State University, 2010: "We Fill Our Pockets"

Plainsongs: "Without Supervision"

Playa, Playa at Summer Lake Anthology, 2019: "Vista"

Poets & Artists: "Climate Song"

Right Hand Pointing: "Driving Home From Work"

San Pedro River Review: "Bringing You Home," "The Day Father's Shop Burned to the Ground"

The Smoking Poet: "Roadside Memo: Jasmine"

Susuin Valley Review: "Parhelion," "Rest of Our Lives"

Verseweavers: "Our Own Private Alaska"

Walloon Writers Review: "Grandpa's Gun," "Lake Effect"

Writing the Land: Currents, NatureCulture, 2024: "Confluence"

"The Day Father's Shop Burned to the Ground" was a Semi-Finalist in *Nimrod International's* 2008 Pablo Neruda Poetry Prize Competition, and along with "Grandpa's Gun," also appear in *Some Weather*, Plain View Press, 2008 (out of print).

"History, The Homemaker" was a semifinalist in *Crab Creek Review's* 2017 Poetry Prize Contest.

"Home Ground (Chromium Tahoe)," "Ramona Falls," and "Great Basin" are in the limited edition chapbook *Untitled Country*, Pudding House Publications, 2009 (out of print).

"Our Own Private Alaska," a collaboration with the poet Kristin Berger (permission granted), received Second Prize in the Oregon Poetry Association's 2012 annual contest and appears in *How Light Reaches Us*, Kristin Berger, Aldrich Press, 2016.

"Patient and Helper," "We Fill Our Pockets," "Parhelion (Sundog)," "Four Tenses," and "History, The Homemaker" are in the chapbook *Daughters, Here Daughters, Gone*, Uttered Chaos Press, 2018.

"Samsara" and "Stowaway" first appeared in *The Constellation of Extinct Stars and Other Poems*, Salmon Poetry, 2016.

Gratitude

Thank you to John Albiso for creating and sustaining the Sally Albiso Poetry Book Award, Lana Hechtman Ayers, Managing Editor of MoonPath Press, for her support, and Tonya Namura for her beautiful design of this book.

With gratitude for Playa at Summer Lake and Oregon State University's Spring Creek Project, whose fellowship-residency awards have helped sustain my creative work over the years.

Thank you to Writing the Land, and land trusts and conservation organizations everywhere. A special shout-out to the California Tahoe Conservancy, Columbia Land Trust (Oregon-Washington), Cowiche Canyon Conservancy (Washington), Little Traverse Conservancy (Michigan), McKenzie River Trust (Oregon), Metro Open Spaces (Portland, OR), and the Oregon Natural Desert Association, whose environmental stewardship efforts and the special places they care for have inspired my writing.

With love for my daughters, Caroline and Lianne, parents, Diane and Frederick, sister, Stacey, and partner and fellow poet, Kristin. Thank you to Kristin and her mom, Carol, as well, for reopening the portal to northern Michigan, the home ground that our families share.

About the Author

Scot Siegel, recipient of the 2024 Sally Albiso Poetry Book Award, is a city planner, educator, and author of three chapbooks and four full-length poetry collections, including *Tender Currencies*. Previous volumes include *The Constellation of Extinct Stars and Other Poems* (2016) and *Thousands Flee California Wildflowers* (2012) from Salmon Poetry.

Siegel works with *Writing the Land*, which pairs poets with land trusts nationwide. He received the Oregon Poetry Association Poet's Choice Award, and the late US Poet Laureate Philip Levine recognized Siegel's long poem "Pages Torn From a Schoolmarm's Diary" as Finalist with Honorable Mention in *Nimrod International's* 2012 Pablo Neruda Poetry Prize Competition.

Siegel's poems appear in many journals and are part of the permanent public art installation along TriMet's Light Rail Orange Line in Portland, Oregon. He has received fellowship residencies with Playa at Summer Lake and Oregon State University's Spring Creek Project. www.scotsiegel.com

More Praise for *Tender Curiences*

Scot Siegel's poems in *Tender Currencies* are achingly beautiful meditations on nature and degradation, postponed-but-now-present love, and the complexities of family history. Poems like "Transpiration" and "The Blue Whale and Her Diamonds" require us to wrestle with the damage wrought by invasive species while acknowledging their undeniable beauty and the extra-worldly quality of their journeys. These poems also carry hope for restoration, as in "Confluence," where the reader imagines "the brown blur of an otter in the glimmer / of midday sun" only to realize the river must be unstraightened, as it soon will be, to once again become an attractive home for wildlife.

All of the poems in *Tender Currencies* are love poems in one way or another. In "Ramona Falls," Siegel asks the reader "what is love/if not a freefall/forestalled"? These deft, contemplative poems will leave readers enriched, inspired, and hopeful as they continue to mull the book's many wise and urgent questions.

—Ann Tweedy, author of *Beleaguered Oases* and *The Body's Alphabet* winner of the Bisexual Book Award in Poetry and the Human Relations Indie Book Award

Scot Siegel's speaker in *Tender Currencies* inhabits at least two worlds, one with smart phones and weather apps, the other with buntings and their "a sweet-swishing-melodic-squeegee song / pine top to pine top." Of these two worlds, it's the natural one (and what's left of it) that most answers to Siegel's presence and regard—that wish to stay in touch, or, as in "Home Ground," to be immersed in 40°F lake water that wakes the heart.

Tender Currencies steadies the spirit. It stays keenly aware of language and sound. It proceeds exactly as its title implies, paying attention, gathering its wisdoms, affirming that "History knows the homeless are royalty. / She keeps the leftovers warm for centuries. / History is never alone. / Her secret lover wears the old cologne. / History leaves the door open." And in the end, this book finds love in hand and voice.

—Lex Runciman, author of
Salt Moons: Poems 1981-2016

www.ingramcontent.com/pod-product-compliance
Lightning Source LLC
LaVergne TN
LVHW041619070526
838199LV00052B/3199